Pebble™ Plus

Under the Sea

Seals

by Carol K. Lindeen

Consulting Editor: Gail Saunders-Smith, PhD
Consultant: Jody Rake, Member
Southwest Marine/Aquatic Educators' Association

Capstone press

Mankato, Minnesota

Pebble Plus is published by Capstone Press,
151 Good Counsel Drive, P.O. Box 669, Mankato, Minnesota 56002.
www.capstonepress.com

1 2 3 4 5 6 10 09 08 07 06 05

Library of Congress Cataloging-in-Publication Data
Lindeen, Carol K., 1976–
    Seals / by Carol K. Lindeen.
    p. cm.—(Pebble Plus—Under the Sea)
    Includes bibliographical references and index.
    ISBN 0-7368-3663-2 (hardcover)
    1. Seals (Animals)—Juvenile literature. I. Title. II. Series.
QL737.P64L556 2005
599.79—dc22   2004011101

Summary: Simple text and photographs present seals, their body parts, and their behavior.

Editorial Credits
Martha E. H. Rustad, editor; Juliette Peters, set designer; Kate Opseth, book designer; Kelly Garvin,
    photo researcher; Scott Thoms, photo editor

Photo Credits
Corbis/Galen Rowell, 6–7
Digital Vision/Joel Simon, 1
Francois Gohier, cover
Minden Pictures/Flip Nicklin, 12–13; Frans Lanting, 4–5
Seapics.com/Ursus/Bob Cranston, 20–21; Goran Ehlme, 14–15; Howard Hall, 16–17; James D. Watt, 8–9;
    Richard Herrmann, 18–19; Roy Tanami, 10–11

Note to Parents and Teachers

The Under the Sea set supports national science standards related to the diversity and
unity of life. This book describes and illustrates seals. The images support early readers
in understanding the text. The repetition of words and phrases helps early readers learn
new words. This book also introduces early readers to subject-specific vocabulary words,
which are defined in the Glossary section. Early readers may need assistance to read
some words and to use the Table of Contents, Glossary, Read More, Internet Sites, and
Index sections of the book.

Table of Contents

What Are Seals?

Seals are mammals
with flippers. Seals live
in and near the sea.

Large seals are longer
than a tall person.
Small seals are as long
as a child.

Body Parts

Seals have flippers.

Flippers help seals swim.

flipper

Seals have fur and blubber.

Fur and blubber help seals

stay warm.

Seals have whiskers.

Whiskers help seals

find food.

What Seals Do

Seals dive to hunt.

Seals eat fish

and other animals.

Seals can stay under
the water for a long time.
They swim up to the surface
to breathe.

Seals rest on the shore.

They stay warm in the sun.

Under the Sea

Seals live on the shore
and under the sea.

Glossary

blubber—a thick layer of fat under the skin of some animals; blubber keeps animals warm.

dive—to go down into the water headfirst

flipper—a flat limb with bones on the bodies of some animals; seals use their flippers to swim.

fur—the thick, hairy coat covering the bodies of some animals

mammal—a warm-blooded animal that breathes air; mammals have hair or fur; female mammals feed milk to their young.

shore—the land next to a body of water

surface—the outside or outermost layer of something

whisker—a long hair near the mouth of an animal

Read More

Hewett, Joan. *A Harbor Seal Pup Grows Up.* Baby Animals. Minneapolis: Carolrhoda Books, 2002.

Lynch, Wayne. *Seals.* Our Wild World. Minnetonka, Minn.: NorthWord Press, 2002.

Rustad, Martha E. H. *Seals.* Ocean Life. Mankato, Minn.: Pebble Books, 2001.

Townsend, Emily Rose. *Seals.* Polar Animals. Mankato, Minn.: Pebble Books, 2004.

Internet Sites

FactHound offers a safe, fun way to find Internet sites related to this book. All of the sites on FactHound have been researched by our staff.

Here's how:

1. Visit *www.facthound.com*

2. Type in this special code **0736836632** for age-appropriate sites. Or enter a search word related to this book for a more general search.

3. Click on the **Fetch It** button.

FactHound will fetch the best sites for you!

Index

Word Count: 103
Grade Level: 1
Early-Intervention Level: 10